Fresh Kills

Elyzabeth Gregory Wilder

Methuen Drama

Published by Methuen 2004

1 3 5 7 9 10 8 6 4 2

First published in 2004 by
Methuen Publishing Limited
215 Vauxhall Bridge Road
London SW1V 1EJ

Methuen Publishing Limited Reg. No. 3543167

A CIP catalogue record for this book is available
from the British Library

ISBN 0 413 77493 7

Typeset by Country Setting, Kingsdown, Kent
Printed and bound in Great Britain by
Cox and Wyman Ltd, Reading, Berkshire

Caution

ROYAL COURT

Royal Court Theatre presents

FRESH KILLS

by **Elyzabeth Gregory Wilder**

First performance at the Royal Court Jerwood Theatre Upstairs,
Sloane Square, London on 5 November 2004.

FRESH KILLS is presented as part of the YOUNG PLAYWRIGHTS' SEASON 2004,
a Genesis Project.

FRESH KILLS

by **Elyzabeth Gregory Wilder**

Cast
Eddie **Phil Daniels**
Marie **Nicola Walker**
Nick **John Sharian**
Arnold **Matt Smith**

Director **Wilson Milam**
Designer **Ultz**
Lighting Designers **Ultz, Trevor Wallace**
Sound Designer **Scott Myers**
Assistant Designers **Jeremy Daker, Elizabeth K Schwartz**
Casting **Lisa Makin**
Production Manager **Paul Handley**
Stage Managers **Rachel Barkataki, Dani Youngman**
Costume Supervisor **Jackie Orton**
Dialect Coach **Kate Godfrey**
Company Voice Work **Patsy Rodenburg**

The Royal Court would like to thank the following for their help with this production: Durfee Foundation, Jose Rivera, New York University, Youngblood.

THE COMPANY

Elyzabeth Gregory Wilder (writer)
Theatre includes: Tales of an Adolescent Fruit Fly,
The First Day of Hunting Season, In Ocean Springs,
The Theory of Relativity, The Spirit of Ecstasy
(Ensemble Studio Theater/Ergo Theatre/Alabama
Shakespeare Festival/Barter Theater).
Awards include: Prism Generation Next Screen
Writing Fellowship, Tennessee Williams Playwriting
Scholarship, Dakin Playwriting Fellowship, Next
Step Playwriting Fellowship, MacDowell Fellowship.
Elyzabeth is a member of Youngblood, the Ensemble
Studio Theater's program for writers under 30.

Jeremy Daker (assistant designer)
For the Royal Court: Bone, The Weather, Bear Hug.
Other theatre includes; L'Elisir D'Amore (Trioler
Landes); When Harry Met Sally (Theatre Royal,
Haymarket); Hobson's Choice (Young Vic); Daphne
(Lincoln Centre, NY); Gotterdamerung (Brazil);
Seven Doors, Three Women and a Piano Tuner,
Holes in the Skin (Minerva); Macbeth (Dundee);
Sergeant Musgrave's Dance, Home (Oxford Stage
Co); Release the Beat (Arcola); Singer (Tricylce);
Broken Fiction (Linbury Studio); Richard III (RSC);
Twilight of the Gods (ENO); The Seagull
(Chichester Festival).
As a designer: Ministry of Pleasure (Latchmere);
Lear (RNT Studio); Comedy of Vanity
(Union/Edinburgh festival).
Jeremy was a finalist in the 2003 Linbury Prize.

Phil Daniels
For the Royal Court: Heros, Class Enemy, Tibetan
Inroads.
Other theatre includes: True West (Bristol Old Vic);
The Green Man (Theatre Royal, Plymouth/Bush);
A Winter's Tale (RNT); Dealer's Choice
(RNT/Vaudeville); Carousel (RNT/West End);
The Closing Number (Hampstead); Johnny Oil
Strikes Back (Edinburgh/Soho); The Lucky Ones
(Stratford East); The Merchant of Venice, The Jew of
Malta, Measure for Measure, The Revenger's
Tragedy, A Clockwork Orange (RSC); Rosencrantz
and Guildenstern are Dead (Young Vic/Hong Kong).
Television includes: Outlaws, Waking the Dead,
The Long Firm, Time Gentlemen Please, Sex, Chips
& Rock 'n Roll, Stand and Deliver, Sex and
Chocolate, Sunnyside Farm, Holding On, One Foot
in the Grave, Miss Julie, Rick Mayall Presents,
Will You Love Me Tomorrow?, Pickwick Papers,
Meantime, A Midsummer Night's Dream, Out of
Mecca - The Bride, Glitter, Hanging Around, Raven,
Four Idle Hands, Molly Wopsies.
Film includes: Goodbye Charlie Bright, Nasty
Neighbours, Bad Behaviour, Billy the Kid and the
Green Baize Vampire, The Bride, Breaking Glass,
Scum, Quadrophenia, Zulu Dawn, The Class of Miss
McMichael.

Wilson Milam (director)
For the Royal Court: Flesh Wound (& Galway Arts
Festival).
Theatre includes (UK and Ireland): Defender of the
Faith (Abbey, Dublin); True West (Bristol Old Vic);
Mr. Placebo (Traverse); Lieutenant of Inishmore
(RSC Stratford/Barbican/Garrick/tour); On Such As
We (Abbey, Dublin); A Lie of the Mind (Donmar);
The Wexford Trilogy (Tricycle/Lowry/Gateway);
Hurlyburly (Old Vic/Queen's); Bug (Gate, London);
Killer Joe (Traverse/Bush/Vaudeville).
US theatre includes: Closer (Berkeley Rep); Bug
(Woolly Mammoth, Washington DC); Killer Joe
(Soho Playhouse/29th St. Rep, New York/Next
Theater, Chicago); Pot Mom (Steppenwolf,
Chicago); Caine Mutiny Court-Martial (A Red
Orchid, Chicago); Skeleton (Shattered Globe,
Chicago).
Television includes: Dr. Who-Scream of the Shalka.

Scott Myers
Theatre includes: Sea of Tranquility, Writer's Block,
The Night Heron, Blue/Orange, Dublin Carol,
Frame 312, This Thing of Darkness (Atlantic, NY);
Recent Tragic Events, Psych, The Credeaux Canvas
(Playwrights Horizons, NY); The Violet Hour
(Biltmore, NY); The Miracle Worker (Charlotte
Rep., N.Carolina); The Crucible (Virginia Theatre,
NY); Further Than The Furthest Thing (Manhattan
Theatre Club, NY); A Winter's Tale, Love's Labour's
Lost, Julius Caesar, Richard II (Chicago Shakespeare
Theatre); Mornings at Seven (Lincoln Center at the
Lyceum/Ahmanson, LA); Left (NY Stage and Film
Festival); An Almost Holy Picture (Roundabout,
NY); Speaking in Tongues (Gramercy Theatre, NY);
Madame Melville (The Promenade, NY/Vaudeville,
London); The Blue Room (The Cort, NY/Donmar);
Amy's View (Lincoln Center, NY); A Doll's House
(Belasco, NY); Racing Demon, Arcadia (Vivian
Beaumont, NY); The Novice (Almeida); The Fall
Guy, Tobaccoland, King Lear, The Deep Blue Sea,
Crimes of the Heart, The Misfits (Royal Exchange,
Manchester); On the Razzle (Chichester Festival);
Roll Over Jehovah (New End); Hard Times, Miss
Julie (Theatre Royal, Haymarket); Side Man,
Personals (Apollo); Arcadia (Chichester Festival);
Henry IV,-Parts I and II, The Lion, The Witch and
the Wardrobe, In The Company Of Men, The White
Devil (RSC); The Lady In The Van (Queen's);
Billy Liar, Women of Troy, The Prime Of Miss Jean
Brodie, Peter Pan, Amy's View, Inadmissible
Evidence, Arcadia, Ma Rainey's Black Bottom,
The Madness Of George III, Absence of War, Racing
Demon, The Trilogy, Richard III, The Voysey
Inheritance, Napoli Millionaria, John Gabriel
Borkman, La Grande Magia, Sweet Bird of Youth,
Johnny on a Spot (RNT); The Invention of Love
(RNT/Theatre Royal, Haymarket); A Doll's House

(Comedy); The Glass Menagerie (Comedy/Donmar); The Eleventh Commandment, The Positive Hour (Hampstead).
Film includes: They Only Came Out At Night, Second Thoughts, The Last Starfighter, Jinxed, Sundance, Terminator.
Television includes: Perfectly Frank, Charlie's Aunt, Your Choice for the Film Awards, Best of Broadway, Red Skeleton's Funny Faces, Rich Little, National Crime and Violence, Miss California Beauty Pageants.

Elizabeth K Schwartz (assistant designer)
Elizabeth is assisting Ultz whilst studying in London on a theatre foreign study program. She attends Dartmouth College in Hanover, New Hampshire.

John Sharian
For the Royal Court: The Sweetest Swing in Baseball, Faith, The One You Love.
Other theatre includes: Action (Young Vic); A Streetcar Named Desire, All My Sons, Lone Stars & PVT Wars, The Life & Death of a Buffalo Soldier, The Hairy Ape (Bristol Old Vic); Life During Wartime (Lyric Studio); Macbeth (York Theatre); A Lie of the Mind (BAC); A View from the Bridge (York Theatre Royal); Laundry Room at the Hotel Madrid (Gate); Small Craft Warnings (Manchester Library); Hamlet (Shaw Theatre); Entertaining Mr Sloane, Who's Afraid of Virginia Woolf, Safe Sex, The Importance of Being Earnest, Curse of the Starving Class, A Streetcar Named Desire (New Ehrlich Theatre, USA); As You Like It, American Buffalo, Servant of Two Masters, Getting Out (Kenyon Festival, USA); No End of Blame, The Castle (Playwrights' Platform USA); Two for the Seesaw, Harvey, Fifth of July (Tufts Arena Stage, USA); Macbeth (American Rep. Theatre); Baal, The Taming of the Shrew (Boston Stage Company).
Television includes: Sex Traffik, Small Potatoes, Chicken Ruin, Crocodile Shoes, Dead Men's Tales, Red Dwarf.
Film includes: Jason & the Argonauts, Do Not Disturb, Fortress 2, New World Disorder, 24 Hours in London, Saving Private Ryan, Lost in Space, Fifth Element, Death Machine, Two Sane Men, The Machinist, Calendar Girls.
Radio includes: Titanic Enquiries, Man of All Work.

Matt Smith
Theatre includes: The Master and the Margarita, Murder in the Cathedral (NYT).
Television includes: Watch Over Me.
Fresh Kills is Matt's professional debut on stage.

Ultz (designer and lighting designer)
As designer, for the Royal Court: Young Playwrights' Season 2004, Fallout, The Night Heron, Fireface, Lift Off, Mojo (& Steppenwolf, Chicago).
As designer, theatre includes: sixteen productions for the RSC including Good (& Broadway), The Art of Success (also at Manhattan Theatre Club); The Black Prince, Me and Mamie O'Rourke, A Madhouse in Goa, Animal Crackers, When Harry Met Sally (West End); Slavs! (Hampstead); The Resistible Rise of Arturo Ui, Ramayana (RNT); Hobson's Choice (Young Vic); Xerxes, La Clemenza di Tito, The Rake's Progress, Die Entführung aus dem Serail (Bavarian State Opera).
As director and designer, other theatre includes: Summer Holiday (Blackpool Opera House, London Apollo, UK tour, South African tour); Jesus Christ Superstar (Aarhus and Copenhagen); Don Giovanni, Cosi Fan Tutte (in Japanese for Tokyo Globe); A Midsummer Night's Dream (National Arts Centre, Ottawa); Dragon (RNT); The Screens (California); The Maids, Deathwatch (co-directed RSC); The Blacks (co-directed Market Theatre Johannesburg and Stockholms Stadsteater); Perikles (Stockholms Stadsteater); Snowbull (Hampstead); L'Elisir D'Amore (Tiroler Landes Theater); The Public, The Taming of the Shrew, Pericles, Baiju Bawra, Da Boyz (Theatre Royal, Stratford East).

Nicola Walker
For the Royal Court: Sweetheart, The Man of Mode/The Libertine (with Out of Joint) Hated Nightfall.
Other theatre includes: Tales from the Vienna Woods, Edmond, Free (RNT); Modern Dance for Beginners (Soho); The Dead Eye Boy (Hampstead); Sexual Perversity in Chicago (Sheffield Crucible); A Lie of the Mind, Passion Play (Donmar & Comedy); Fifty Revolutions (Oxford Stage); Party Tricks (Nottingham Playhouse); The Lovers (Gate & tour).
Television includes: Spooks, People Like Us, Dalziel and Pascoe, The Last Train, Jonathan Creek, Touching Evil, Chalk, A Dance to the Music of Time, Cows, Moll Flanders.
Film includes: Shooting Dogs, Shiner, Four Weddings and a Funeral.
Radio includes: La Grande Therese, The Big Town All Stars, Now We are Four.

Trevor Wallace (lighting designer)
For the Royal Court: Bone, Notes on Falling Leaves, Rampage, A Day in Dull Armour, Graffiti.
Other theatre includes: Golden Boy, Nobody's Perfect, The Book of the Banshee, Kit and the Widow - The Fat Lady Sings (Yvonne Arnaud); Cabaret, Sweet Charity (Electric, Guildford); The Changeling (Sandpit, St Albans); The Weir (Theatro Technis); Comedy of Errors, Grimm Tales, Richard III, Cyrano de Bergerac, Les Enfants du Paradis, A Midsummer Night's Dream (Minack).

THE ENGLISH STAGE COMPANY AT THE ROYAL COURT

The English Stage Company at the Royal Court opened in 1956 as a subsidised theatre producing new British plays, international plays and some classical revivals.

The first artistic director George Devine aimed to create a writers' theatre, 'a place where the dramatist is acknowledged as the fundamental creative force in the theatre and where the play is more important than the actors, the director, the designer'. The urgent need was to find a contemporary style in which the play, the acting, direction and design are all combined. He believed that 'the battle will be a long one to continue to create the right conditions for writers to work in'.

Devine aimed to discover 'hard-hitting, uncompromising writers whose plays are stimulating, provocative and exciting'. The Royal Court production of John Osborne's Look Back in Anger in May 1956 is now seen as the decisive starting point of modern British drama and the policy created a new generation of British playwrights. The first wave included John Osborne, Arnold Wesker, John Arden, Ann Jellicoe, N F Simpson and Edward Bond. Early seasons included new international plays by Bertolt Brecht, Eugène Ionesco, Samuel Beckett, Jean-Paul Sartre and Marguerite Duras.

The theatre started with the 400-seat proscenium arch Theatre Downstairs, and in 1969 opened a second theatre, the 60-seat studio Theatre Upstairs. Some productions transfer to the West End, such as Terry Johnson's Hitchcock Blonde, Caryl Churchill's Far Away and Conor McPherson's The Weir. Recent touring productions include Sarah Kane's 4.48 Psychosis (US tour) and Ché Walker's Flesh Wound (Galway Arts Festival). The Royal Court also co-produces plays which have transferred to the West End or toured internationally, such as Conor McPherson's Shining City (with Gate Theatre, Dublin), Sebastian Barry's The Steward of Christendom and Mark Ravenhill's Shopping and Fucking (with Out of Joint), Martin McDonagh's The Beauty Queen Of Leenane (with Druid), Ayub Khan Din's East is East (with Tamasha).

Since 1994 the Royal Court's artistic policy has again been vigorously directed to finding and producing a new generation of playwrights. The writers include Joe Penhall, Rebecca Prichard, Michael Wynne, Nick Grosso, Judy Upton, Meredith Oakes, Sarah Kane, Anthony Neilson, Judith Johnson, James Stock, Jez Butterworth, Marina Carr, Phyllis Nagy, Simon Block, Martin

photo: Andy Chopping

McDonagh, Mark Ravenhill, Ayub Khan Din, Tamantha Hammerschlag, Jess Walters, Ché Walker, Conor McPherson, Simon Stephens, Richard Bean, Roy Williams, Gary Mitchell, Mick Mahoney, Rebecca Gilman, Christopher Shinn, Kia Corthron, David Gieselmann, Marius von Mayenburg, David Eldridge, Leo Butler, Zinnie Harris, Grae Cleugh, Roland Schimmelpfennig, DeObia Oparei, Enda Walsh, Vassily Sigarev, the Presnyakov Brothers, Marcos Barbosa, Lucy Prebble, John Donnelly and Clare Pollard. This expanded programme of new plays has been made possible through the support of A.S.K. Theater Projects and the Skirball Foundation, The Jerwood Charity, the American Friends of the Royal Court Theatre and many in association with the National Theatre Studio.

In recent years there have been record-breaking productions at the box office, with capacity houses for Joe Penhall's Dumb Show, Conor McPherson's Shining City, Roy Williams' Fallout and Terry Johnson's Hitchcock Blonde.

The refurbished theatre in Sloane Square opened in February 2000, with a policy still inspired by the first artistic director George Devine. The Royal Court is an international theatre for new plays and new playwrights, and the work shapes contemporary drama in Britain and overseas.

AWARDS FOR ROYAL COURT

Jez Butterworth won the 1995 George Devine Award, the Writers' Guild New Writer of the Year Award, the Evening Standard Award for Most Promising Playwright and the Olivier Award for Best Comedy for Mojo.

The Royal Court was the overall winner of the 1995 Prudential Award for the Arts for creativity, excellence, innovation and accessibility. The Royal Court Theatre Upstairs won the 1995 Peter Brook Empty Space Award for innovation and excellence in theatre.

Michael Wynne won the 1996 Meyer-Whitworth Award for The Knocky. Martin McDonagh won the 1996 George Devine Award, the 1996 Writers' Guild Best Fringe Play Award, the 1996 Critics' Circle Award and the 1996 Evening Standard Award for Most Promising Playwright for The Beauty Queen of Leenane. Marina Carr won the 19th Susan Smith Blackburn Prize (1996/7) for Portia Coughlan. Conor McPherson won the 1997 George Devine Award, the 1997 Critics' Circle Award and the 1997 Evening Standard Award for Most Promising Playwright for The Weir. Ayub Khan Din won the 1997 Writers' Guild Awards for Best West End Play and Writers' Guild New Writer of the Year and the 1996 John Whiting Award for East is East (co-production with Tamasha).

At the 1998 Tony Awards, Martin McDonagh's The Beauty Queen of Leenane (co-production with Druid Theatre Company) won four awards including Garry Hynes for Best Director and was nominated for a further two. Eugene Ionesco's The Chairs (co-production with Theatre de Complicite) was nominated for six Tony awards. David Hare won the 1998 Time Out Live Award for Outstanding Achievement and six awards in New York including the Drama League, Drama Desk and New York Critics Circle Award for Via Dolorosa. Sarah Kane won the 1998 Arts Foundation Fellowship in Playwriting. Rebecca Prichard won the 1998 Critics' Circle Award for Most Promising Playwright for Yard Gal (co-production with Clean Break).

Conor McPherson won the 1999 Olivier Award for Best New Play for The Weir. The Royal Court won the 1999 ITI Award for Excellence in International Theatre. Sarah Kane's Cleansed was judged Best Foreign Language Play in 1999 by Theater Heute in Germany. Gary Mitchell won the 1999 Pearson Best Play Award for Trust. Rebecca Gilman was joint winner of the 1999 George Devine Award and won the 1999 Evening Standard Award for Most Promising Playwright for The Glory of Living.

In 1999, the Royal Court won the European theatre prize New Theatrical Realities, presented at Taormina Arte in Sicily, for its efforts in recent years in discovering and producing the work of young British dramatists.

Roy Williams and Gary Mitchell were joint winners of the George Devine Award 2000 for Most Promising Playwright for Lift Off and The Force of Change respectively. At the Barclays Theatre Awards 2000 presented by the TMA, Richard Wilson won the Best Director Award for David Gieselmann's Mr Kolpert and Jeremy Herbert won the Best Designer Award for Sarah Kane's 4.48 Psychosis. Gary Mitchell won the Evening Standard's Charles Wintour Award 2000 for Most Promising Playwright for The Force of Change. Stephen Jeffreys' I Just Stopped by to See the Man won an AT&T: On Stage Award 2000.

David Eldridge's Under the Blue Sky won the Time Out Live Award 2001 for Best New Play in the West End. Leo Butler won the George Devine Award 2001 for Most Promising Playwright for Redundant. Roy Williams won the Evening Standard's Charles Wintour Award 2001 for Most Promising Playwright for Clubland. Grae Cleugh won the 2001 Olivier Award for Most Promising Playwright for Fucking Games. Richard Bean was joint winner of the George Devine Award 2002 for Most Promising Playwright for Under the Whaleback. Caryl Churchill won the 2002 Evening Standard Award for Best New Play for A Number. Vassily Sigarev won the 2002 Evening Standard Charles Wintour Award for Most Promising Playwright for Plasticine. Ian MacNeil won the 2002 Evening Standard Award for Best Design for A Number and Plasticine. Peter Gill won the 2002 Critics' Circle Award for Best New Play for The York Realist (English Touring Theatre). Ché Walker won the 2003 George Devine Award for Most Promising Playwright for Flesh Wound. Lucy Prebble won the 2003 Critics' Circle Award and the 2004 George Devine Award for Most Promising Playwright for The Sugar Syndrome.

ROYAL COURT BOOKSHOP

The Royal Court bookshop offers a diverse selection of contemporary plays and publications on the theory and practice of modern drama. The staff specialise in assisting with the selection of audition monologues and scenes.
Royal Court playtexts from past and present productions cost £2.
The Bookshop is situated in the downstairs
ROYAL COURT BAR AND FOOD.
Monday–Friday 3–10pm, Saturday 2.30–10pm
For information tel: 020 7565 5024
or email: bookshop@royalcourttheatre.com

PROGRAMME SUPPORTERS

The Royal Court (English Stage Company Ltd) receives its principal funding from Arts Council England, London. It is also supported financially by a wide range of private companies and public bodies and earns the remainder of its income from the box office and its own trading activities. The Royal Borough of Kensington & Chelsea gives an annual grant to the Royal Court Young Writers Programme.

The Genesis Foundation supports the International Season and Young Writers Festival.

The Jerwood Charity supports new plays by new playwrights through the Jerwood New Playwrights series. The Skirball Foundation funds a Playwrights' Programme at the theatre. The Artistic Director's Chair is supported by a lead grant from The Peter Jay Sharp Foundation, contributing to the activities of the Artistic Director's office. Bloomberg Mondays, the Royal Court's reduced price ticket scheme, is supported by Bloomberg. Over the past eight years the BBC has supported the Gerald Chapman Fund for directors.

ROYAL COURT
SLOANE SQUARE

Jerwood Theatre Upstairs
YOUNG PLAYWRIGHTS' SEASON 2004

A Genesis Project
www.genesisfoundation.org.uk

26 November– 18 December 7.45pm
A GIRL IN A CAR WITH A MAN

by **Rob Evans**
Directed by
Joe Hill-Gibbins

Cast includes: Mark Bonnar, Claudie Blakley, Mark Leadbetter, Andrew Scott, Sukie Smith
Design: Ultz

Jerwood Theatre Downstairs
28 October– 4 December 7.30pm
FORTY WINKS

by **Kevin Elyot**
Directed by **Katie Mitchell**

Cast: Anastasia Hille, Stephen Kennedy, Carey Mulligan, Paul Ready, Dominic Rowan, Simon Wilson
Design: Hildegard Bechtler
Lighting: Paule Constable
Sound: Gareth Fry

BOX OFFICE
020 7565 5000
BOOK ONLINE
www.royalcourttheatre.com

ARTS COUNCIL ENGLAND

Fresh Kills

Characters

Eddie
Marie
Nick
Arnold

Act One

Scene One

Lights rise on an old pick-up truck. **Eddie**, *a blue-collar guy in his thirties, is on the brink of a mind-blowing orgasm. He grips the steering wheel. His breathing intensifies. He honks the horn.*

Eddie Oh. My. God.

He can't hold back any longer. He collapses onto the steering wheel.

Marie, *Eddie's wife, sits up. She is in her early thirties.*

Marie I told you you'd like it better out here.

Eddie You are amazing.

Eddie *kisses her. She pushes him away.*

Marie Don't.

Eddie I love to taste me on you.

Marie Eddie.

Eddie I taste good, don't I?

Marie Don't be gross.

Eddie Thank you.

Marie Thank you? Since when did you ever say thank you?

Eddie Thank you.

Marie I gave you a blowjob. People don't say thank you for blowjobs.

Eddie They should.

Marie Well, they don't. People say thank you when you tell them their fly's undone or you make them dessert.

Eddie Think of me as dessert. With whipped cream on top.

Marie   Now you're just being disgusting.

Eddie   Come here.

He pulls **Marie** *towards him. He wraps his arms around her.*

Marie   I read in a magazine that re-enacting your first sexual encounter was supposed to be erotic.

Eddie   If that old Ford could talk.

Marie   You'd be in jail, you kinky little bastard.

Eddie   Hey, I think I remember you coming up with a few ideas of your own.

Marie *gets out of the truck. She turns on the lights to reveal the truck is parked in their garage. The truck takes up one half of the garage, while on the other side is a card table, chairs, mini-fridge and a workbench with shelves. This is* **Eddie**'s *palace.*

Eddie   Where are you going?

Marie   I gotta check on Eddie Jr.

Eddie   He's dead to the world, Marie. Come on. (*Gesturing to the truck.*) Come on, back in.

Marie   No. What if he walked in on us?

Eddie   He's not gonna walk in.

Marie   Just to be safe.

Eddie *calls out of the window.*

Eddie   You think next time we might could actually go somewhere?

Marie   You mean like parking?

Eddie   Yeah. Like parking.

Marie   People get arrested for that.

Eddie   Didn't stop us before. Kind of exciting, don't you think? Somebody watching us.

Marie   Nobody needs to see my stretch-marked ass giving you a blowjob.

Eddie   You used to would have done it.

Marie   I'm not fifteen anymore.

Eddie   We could pretend.

Marie   You can pretend. Knock yourself out.

Marie *starts to leave.*

Eddie   Be back soon?

Marie   Give me a minute.

Marie *exits.* **Eddie** *kicks back and enjoys the moment. He gets out of the truck, pants around his ankles and and shuffles over to the rear of the truck. He pulls up his pants.*

There are several cabinet doors loaded into the back of the truck. He pulls them out and starts sanding.

Marie *returns.*

Marie   He's naked again. I don't know how he does it. I ask him in the morning why he takes his clothes off and he doesn't remember a thing.

Eddie   A man's gotta let himself breathe.

Marie   Eddie, he's six.

Eddie   It's a guy thing.

Marie   You gonna hang those doors tomorrow?

Eddie   If I can get them all done in time.

Marie   I can't have people over with no cabinet doors.

Eddie   They aren't going to build themselves. These things take time. Who do you know who'd care one way or the other?

Marie   I have my interview for the Women's League.

Eddie   There you go with that again.

Marie   It means a lot to me, Eddie.

Eddie   You got friends. Why you need to be a part of some league?

Marie   They're not just some league. They're a well respected part of the community. They do good things. And a few new friends never hurt anybody.

Eddie   We don't need to pay people to be your friend.

Marie   Those dues help support the group. They do a lot for the community.

Eddie   What have they ever done for us?

Marie   They redid the Little League field. And the playground. And donated books to the library.

Eddie   My wife's becoming a middle-class Carnegie.

Marie   It's not just paying dues, either. Everyone does a community service project. To show them you care, you know? I was thinking maybe I'd volunteer at a shelter or something. Teach homeless women how to cook.

Eddie   If they're homeless how they gonna cook, huh? They got no stove, no pots and pans.

Marie   For when they're not homeless any more, smart ass.

Eddie   You got better ways to spend your time. And our money.

Marie   It never hurt to give a little something back.

Eddie *tries to kiss her again.*

Eddie   You want me to give a little something back to you? Huh? That what you want?

Marie *pulls away.*

Marie   It's important, Eddie.

Eddie   I'll have it looking nice for you.

Marie You're just saying that. You'll forget.

Eddie I've had a lot on my mind.

Marie You got me on your mind?

Eddie *takes a little too long to answer.*

Eddie Of course.

Marie You shouldn't have to think about it, Eddie.

Eddie I'm not thinking about it.

Marie So you're not thinking of me?

Eddie Would you stop twisting things? I take two seconds to answer your question and you jump my shit.

Marie Don't make this my fault. I tried to make it special for you tonight. Something different.

Eddie And I said thank you.

Marie Asshole.

Eddie Why are you getting all pissed off? We had a nice night. For once since I don't know when.

Marie *starts to leave.*

Eddie Where you going now?

Marie To bed.

Eddie Marie –

Marie You gonna be up late?

Eddie I told Nick I'd meet him down at McKale's when he gets off duty.

Marie You don't need to be out drinking with Nick this time of night.

Eddie Why? 'Cause it's a 'school night'? I'm a big boy, Marie. I can have a couple of beers if I want them. You said you're going to bed.

Marie   Might be nice having you in bed beside me.

Eddie   Come on, baby, don't be that way. I was gonna pick up some more sandpaper so I can finish your cabinets.

Marie   It's past ten.

Eddie   There's a place by Fresh Kills that's open till eleven.

Marie   The one next to the bar?

Eddie   You're the one who's all worried about not having kitchen cabinets. I couldn't give two shits.

Marie   I work hard to keep our house nice and you don't care.

Eddie   I didn't mean it that way.

Marie   That's what you said.

Eddie   I just meant that . . . Forget it.

Marie   Be quiet when you come in.

Marie *exits.* **Eddie** *waits a moment. He grabs his jacket, checks for his keys. He then takes a look at himself in the mirror. He hesitates. Then gets in the truck.*

End of scene.

Scene Two

An abandoned parking lot at the Fresh Kills landfill in Staten Island. **Eddie** *sits in the driver's seat of the truck.* **Arnold**, *a sixteen-year-old, sits in the passenger seat nursing a bottle of Colt 45 beer. He wears a Mets cap and eats McDonald's French fries.*

A dog barks in the distance. **Arnold** *barks back.*

Arnold   Roof! Grrrrr. (*He spits at the dog.*) Bitch.

Eddie   Hey, man, roll up the window. It's cold out there.

Arnold   It's cold in here.

Eddie We're not here for the conversation.

Arnold You weren't afraid to talk online.

Eddie Look, this isn't something I do. So you can cut the small talk.

Arnold But you are, Eddie. You're doing it.

Arnold *makes a move on* **Eddie**. **Eddie** *pulls away*. **Arnold** *takes a long drink of the beer*.

Arnold It was better the way it was, right? You beating off down in the basement. Squinting at the computer screen. Your wife and kids watching TV upstairs.

Eddie I don't have any kids.

Arnold Liar. You tell your son you beat off in the basement while you talk to boys?

Eddie That's not how it is.

Arnold But you get off on it, right?

Eddie Look, I showed up. Like you told me to. Can we just do . . . whatever . . .

Arnold Your wife know you're cheating on her?

Eddie Looking at pictures isn't cheating.

Arnold That's what you tell yourself?

Eddie (*defensively*) I love my wife.

Arnold Chill. We're just getting to know one another.

Eddie I don't want to get to know you. That's not what this is about.

Arnold Come on. You can't tell me you weren't curious? Do you just like little boys or are you an equal opportunity pervert?

Eddie I'm not a pervert.

Arnold You're sitting in a parked car with a kid and a big stiffy growing in your pants.

Eddie *shifts to hide what* **Arnold** *sees.*

Eddie   This was a bad idea.

Arnold   Why not little girls?

Eddie   I don't know.

Arnold   Yes, you do, Eddie. So do you jerk off before or after you fuck your wife? Some guys gotta look at their dirty little pictures before to get them in the mood and others do it after 'cause their wife's a lousy lay.

Eddie *doesn't respond.*

Arnold   I caught my dad jerking off once. Standing in the bathroom, his dick covered with my mom's pink foam shaving gel. He doesn't have a lot of body hair. It just hung there like the skinned neck of a dead chicken. (*Pause.*) You really should have a drink. You'll have more fun.

Eddie   I should take you back to the ferry.

Arnold   I knew this would happen. You really haven't ever done this?

Eddie   No.

Arnold   People always say that it's their first time and I never believe it 'cause everyone online is a big liar. Leave it to me to find the one guy in all of fucking cyberspace who tells the truth.

Eddie   Don't sound so disappointed.

Arnold   You got another beer?

Eddie *pulls another bottle of Colt 45 out of a brown paper bag.*

Arnold   You went all out, didn't you? Special occasion. Buy the good stuff.

Eddie   Gets the job done.

Arnold *sticks his head out of the window and yells.*

Arnold   Hello? Is anybody out there?

Eddie   Hey man, stop it.

Arnold   What?

Eddie   Somebody might hear.

Arnold   You said they closed this place. Gonna make it into a park or something.

Eddie   Still. You never know.

Arnold   I never been to Staten Island before. My father calls it common. He's a fascist.

Eddie   Sorry I can't give you the full tour.

Arnold   It stinks here, man. Does it stink like this all the time?

Eddie   It's the dump. It's not supposed to smell good.

Arnold   It true Fresh Kills is so big you can see it in outer space?

Eddie   Yeah, they got that printed on all the brochures. Staten Island, the trashiest place on earth.

Arnold   Very romantic. Where'd you take your wife on your first date, the morgue?

Arnold *crumples the bag from the beer and tosses it out the window.*

Eddie   Hey, don't do that.

Arnold   Dude, we're in a dump. Look, I gotta be home by midnight. So we should do something, right? Don't you want to do something?

Arnold *makes another move on* **Eddie**. **Eddie** *pushes him away.*

Eddie   Not like that, man. Not like that.

Arnold   If I wanted to be ignored I could've just stayed home. You want to do something or not?

Eddie   I didn't know it was going to be about this.

Arnold   What did you think it was about? You were looking at dirty pictures of little boys.

Eddie   People send that stuff all the time. Doesn't mean anything.

Arnold   But you decided to take a peek.

Eddie   I changed my mind, OK?

Arnold   You're pathetic, man. Why don't you go home and do your wife? 'Cause you don't have the balls to be here.

Eddie   Shut up. Just shut your face.

Arnold   That get a rise out of you? Pussy.

Eddie   Stop it.

Arnold   Pansy-ass motherfucker.

Eddie   I said shut the fuck up.

Arnold   That turn you on? Get you hot? What do you want? What? Tell me.

Arnold *leans in to kiss* **Eddie***, but* **Eddie** *pulls away.*

Arnold   You wanna kiss me? Huh?

Eddie   No.

Arnold *(tries again)*   Is that it? *(Tries again.)* What if I say please?

Eddie   Get offa me, man.

Arnold *grabs* **Eddie** *and kisses him.* **Eddie** *tries to push him away. He wipes his mouth.*

Arnold   You taste good. The first guy I ever kissed was gross. Bad teeth. I was in Junior High and he offered me a ride home from school. He gave me a joint to smoke, then he put his tongue down my throat. Like I didn't even know what happened. I could taste the pot and the burger he had for lunch and the gum he chewed to hide the smell. And he pulled my hand to his crotch and all I could feel was hot and hard. His balls heavy and tight from the tension. But soft. Like an orange. Like a week old orange rolling round and round in my hands. Relax, man.

Eddie   I can't.

Arnold   I know it ain't the Plaza. You thinking about your kid? About what if one day he found his way to a dark parking lot and the arms of a perv like you?

Eddie   Shut up.

Arnold   Letting some hairy motherfucker cop a feel on his fresh virgin ass?

Eddie *grabs* **Arnold** *by the throat and pins him against the seat.*

Eddie   I said shut the fuck up.

Arnold *starts to laugh.*

Arnold   Now you're getting kinky.

Eddie   Don't talk about my kid.

Arnold   Sorry, man.

Eddie   You gotta go.

Arnold   Remember what we talked about.

Eddie   You got nothing on me. I haven't done anything.

Arnold   You're sitting in a parked car with a minor. Doesn't look so good. Especially if I tell them how you put the moves on me.

Eddie   You little bastard.

Arnold   You play along and everyone gets to have a good time. No harm done.

Eddie *pulls out his wallet and starts rummaging for bills. He pulls out a twenty.*

Eddie   Here. Take this. Take it!

Arnold I don't take money.

Eddie Please.

Arnold Taking money makes me a whore. Twenty bucks makes me a cheap whore. You keep your little money. Buy your kid a Happy Meal.

Eddie *is almost in tears.*

Eddie Please. Goddamn it. Just take the money.

Arnold You got a lot of things I want, Eddie. And when I want it, I'll get it.

Eddie *starts the truck. He turns on the radio very loud and drives.*

End of scene.

Scene Three

The next day. **Eddie***'s garage. The truck is parked on one side. The cabinets sit untouched from the night before.*

Eddie *is cleaning out his truck. He looks tired and worn, but there is a nervous energy about him.* **Nick***, thirties, is a NYPD cop, and a little rough around the edges. He drinks a beer while they talk.*

Nick I'm standing at the toilet with Joey last night, taking a leak. And he's peeing all over himself. And the floor. And my new boots. And I'm like, 'Hey, man, you've got to aim that sucker better.' He looks up at me and he says, 'Daddy, it's not a sucker.' And I think to myself, 'One day, my son. One day you'll wish it was a candy-coated blow pop.' (**Nick** *starts to shuffle a deck of cards.*) I look at Joey and I think, kid, I hope you got it better than me one day. I just smiled at him, and then I showed him how to hold himself and aim. There we were, father and son. Dicks in hand. Taking a piss.

Eddie That's real sweet.

Nick Says he wants to be a cop like his dad. I say God help us all if that boy ever has a gun. I never seen anybody with such bad aim.

Nick *picks up a Mets cap that* **Eddie**'s *discarded from the truck.*

Nick   Since when do you root for the Mets?

Eddie   One of the guys must have left it in the truck.

Eddie *grabs the hat from him and throws it in the garbage.*

Nick   I wouldn't let nobody who was a Mets fan in my truck. You don't need to be associating with that element of society.

Eddie   It's a hat.

Nick   I'm just saying. It's like sacrilege. We oughta burn it right now.

Eddie *throws out a bag from McDonald's and two bottles of beer from the night before. He drops one of the bottles.*

Eddie   Shit.

Nick   Calm down, big guy. What's up with you today? You look like ass.

Eddie   Just tired.

Nick   You gotta stop watching that late-night porn. Didn't your mama ever tell you it'd make you go blind?

Eddie   Couldn't sleep. You want another beer?

Nick   Yeah.

Eddie *pulls out a Colt 45.*

Eddie   Here you go.

Nick   Colt 45. Where you been hanging out, homeboy?

Eddie   It was on sale.

Nick   Didn't know times was so tight for you.

Eddie   I'm sorry. You too good for my beer? Pardon me.

Nick   Gimme the goddamn beer.

Eddie *takes a seat at the table.* **Nick** *deals the cards.*

Nick   Had one of these bottles come through the window of my squad car last week.

Eddie   Who'd you piss off this time?

Nick   Just doing my job as a 'law enforcement officer'. Protecting our taxpayers. Here. (**Nick** *pulls a piece of paper out of his pocket.*) Give this guy a call. He's looking to remodel his kitchen. Told him you'd give him a fair price.

Eddie   Thanks. Marie's been riding my ass.

Marie *enters.*

Marie   You losers gonna drink beer all night?

Eddie   Thinking about it.

Marie   Have they paid you for that dry-wall job?

Eddie   Good to see you too, honey. How was your day?

Marie   Did they?

Eddie   Monday.

Marie   That's what they said last Monday.

Eddie   They had a family emergency. I cut them some slack.

Marie   We've got a family emergency. It's called food on the table.

Nick   I gave him a lead on a kitchen job.

Marie   I see you didn't finish the cabinets today. Sure did take you a long time to get that sandpaper last night. Or were you two schlumps knocking back beers all night?

Eddie   Nick was buying. I can't say no to his generosity. Right, Nick?

Nick *gives* **Eddie** *a confused look.*

Nick   Yeah.

Marie You're a bad influence on Eddie. I'm not gonna let you boys play together no more.

Eddie I'll finish them this weekend. Promise.

Marie I got no doors on my cabinets.

Eddie I said, this weekend.

Marie This weekend's the Cub Scout camp-out.

Eddie Shit.

Marie Eddie.

Marie *starts digging around a shelf in the garage.*

Eddie Hey, watch it over there.

Marie Where's the tent?

Eddie You're messing everything up.

Marie Oh, excuse me. I didn't realise you had a system.

Eddie Well there is, OK?

Marie I just want to check and make sure everything's in the bag.

Eddie Everything's in the bag, Marie.

Marie Like last time, right? Genius here forgets to double check and ends up in the woods with no stakes to hold the tent down with.

Nick That's pretty funny.

Marie Eddie Jr. was so embarrassed. Came home crying.

Eddie I'll take care of it.

Marie *keeps digging.*

Eddie I said I'd take care of it. Do you gotta ride my ass all the time? I'll take care of the tent. And the clothes. And the food. Like I always do.

Marie   Fine.

Eddie   Fine. I swear, a guy fucks up once and it's like you gotta tattoo it on my forehead as a constant reminder.

Marie   I just want Eddie to have a good time.

Eddie   He'll have a good time. He'll have the best fucking time of his life.

Nick   When do I get to see your uniform?

Eddie   It's a T-shirt. All we have to wear is a T-shirt and a hat.

Nick   Now I'm disappointed.

Eddie   Hey, big guy, why don't you balls up and become a Scout Leader?

Nick   You know I don't do the outdoors. No thanks.

Eddie   Awe, come on. The kids love it.

Nick   Are you kidding? My luck I'll be out in the woods taking a dump and end up with poison ivy on my ass. No thank you.

Eddie   Quality time with Bobby.

Nick   Bobby and I have enough quality time together watching TV.

Eddie *sits down and picks up his cards.*

Eddie   So are you gonna deal the cards or what?

Nick   I been waiting on you.

Marie   Well, don't let me interrupt your high-stakes game.

Eddie   By the end of the night, Nick here'll be paying our mortgage.

Nick   In your dreams, sandman.

Eddie   A man's gotta make a living.

Marie   By all means, don't let me get in the way of you supporting the family.

Eddie   You're the one who wants to go spending money on some Women's League. (*To* **Nick**.) Debbie belong to a Women's League?

Nick   No.

Eddie   See? Debbie doesn't need to buy friends. You girls can go shopping together. Make it your own little club.

Marie   It's not the same. I need something to call my own, Eddie. You got Nick and the guys. Me, I got juice-boxes and Legos.

Eddie   It's good enough for Debbie.

Marie   Fine. You gonna be a dick about it, I'll get my own money to pay for it. Pick up some extra shifts at the diner. There. Fuck you, Eddie.

Marie *starts to leave.*

Nick   Could you be a dear and bring us out a little snack?

Marie   Bite me, big boy.

Nick   Such talk from a lady.

Marie *gives him the finger and exits.*

Nick   What's up with you guys?

Eddie   Same shit.

Nick   I don't remember buying you a beer at McKale's last night.

Eddie   Let it go, Nick.

Nick   You got me lying to my sister, I think I deserve an explanation.

Eddie   I had to go buy sandpaper.

Nick   At night?

Eddie   Yeah.

Nick   You fucking around on her?

Eddie   No.

Nick   Would you tell me?

Eddie   No.

Nick   You know I love ya, Eddie. But she's my sister and I got a genetic obligation to kick your ass if you're doing anything that'll hurt her.

Eddie   If I was getting it someplace else, don't you think I'd be in a better mood?

Nick   I mean it. You two need to get out more.

Eddie   Like when?

Nick   I'm serious. You should bring Eddie over to the house one weekend. We'll keep him. You take Marie down to Atlantic City or something. Show her a good time. Get those old home fires burning again, you know.

Eddie   You know what Marie would do if she found out I was spending money on rooms in Atlantic City?

Nick   She'd love it. You gotta romance a woman every now and then. Remind her why you married her.

Eddie   Why did I marry her?

Nick   You don't mean that. (*Pause.*) You're hitting a slump. We all do.

Eddie   Last week Eddie's sitting at the table with his brand new Playdough having a good time. About a half hour later I realise the green Playdough is missing. I'm looking around. Marie's gonna have my head if she finds this green Playdough stuck to something, you know. Then I notice there's this huge bulge in his pants. So I'm like, 'Hey, man, you got a problem in your pants?' And he says, 'No. Daddy. No problem, just Playdough.' And so I say, 'Hey, man, why do you have Playdough in your pants?' And he says, 'Daddy, it makes my pee-pee feel good.' Can you believe that? So that night, Marie's working at the restaurant and I see this Playdough sitting on the table, and I think, why not. So I try it. And it feels good. Like a perfect fit. It was the best sex I've had in months.

Nick   That's disgusting.

Eddie   I'm telling you, Nick. The kid's on to something.

Nick   It's Playdough.

Eddie   Try it.

Nick   You're warped.

The phone rings from inside the house.

Marie (*offstage*)   Eddie, it's for you.

Eddie   Tell whoever it is that I'm in the middle of a business transaction and I'll call back later.

Marie *enters.*

Marie   I'm your secretary now?

Eddie   Who is it?

Marie   Sounds like a kid. Says his name's Arnold.

End of scene.

Scene Four

The dump. It's late. **Arnold** *and* **Eddie** *sit in the truck.*

Arnold   I want my hat back.

Eddie   I don't have it.

Arnold   My Met's cap. Give it back.

Eddie   I threw it out.

Arnold   You just go throwing out stuff that don't belong to you?

Eddie   You're the one who left it.

Arnold   It's my favourite hat.

Eddie   Fine, I'll get you a new one. Will you leave me alone then?

Arnold *gets out of the truck and sits on the hood of* **Eddie**'s *truck.*

Eddie   Get back in the truck.

Arnold   It's a nice night.

Eddie *gets out of the truck.*

Eddie   I know what you're trying to do.

Arnold   Really?

Eddie   I got nothing to say to you.

Arnold   Your wife sounded kinda sexy on the phone.

Eddie   You can't call me at home.

Arnold   What's your kid's name?

Eddie   None of your business.

Arnold   Now that's no way to be.

Eddie   Leave him alone.

Arnold   You like your kid?

Eddie   Stop it.

Arnold   You love him?

Eddie   Of course I do.

Arnold   Some don't.

Eddie   I love my kid.

Arnold   I figured as much. You see, Eddie, I think behind your tight-ass exterior, you're a pretty OK guy. Am I right? I am.

Eddie   Get offa my truck.

Arnold Come on, Eddie. Sit beside me.

Eddie *tries to pull him off the truck but* **Arnold** *holds on.*

Eddie I said get offa my goddamn truck.

Arnold I'm starting to think you don't like me. Don't you like me, Eddie? Don't you wanna fuck me?

Eddie *opens the door and tries to pop the hood.*

Eddie No.

Eddie *tries to lift the hood.* **Arnold** *goes tumbling backward.*

Arnold Don't you want me to go down on you? Like your wife used to?

Eddie No.

Arnold I'm really good. You don't know what you're missing.

Eddie *is finally able to drag* **Arnold** *off the hood of the truck.* **Arnold** *falls to the ground.*

Arnold If you wanted me on my knees you could've just asked.

Eddie Stop talking like that.

Arnold You like when I talk that way online.

Eddie That's different.

Arnold Why?

Eddie Just is.

Arnold Can't deal with the real thing, can you? This too much for you, Eddie?

Eddie I liked it the way it was.

Arnold When you didn't have to look me in the eye.

Eddie Yes.

Arnold Can't go back now.

Eddie   Why not? It was fun. Nobody got hurt.

Arnold   'Cause I want more than that.

Eddie   Look it. I don't want to talk to you. I don't want to see you. I don't want to be your friend. Or your fuck-buddy.

Arnold   Now that's not nice.

Eddie   I mean it. It was a mistake.

Arnold   I'm a mistake?

Eddie   Yes.

Arnold   I'm not a mistake. You're the mistake. You're the fuck-up here.

Eddie *takes a moment to collect himself.*

Eddie   Just tell me what you want.

Arnold   Just talk to me, man. That's all I'm asking. Let's just talk. That work for you?

Eddie   OK. Fine. We'll talk.

Arnold   Fine.

They sit in silence.

Arnold   What do you and your kid do together?

Eddie   I don't know.

Arnold   Yes you do, Eddie. Talk to me, man. Don't clam up. You stop talking, I'll start talking. Understand? Speak!

Eddie   We play ball. Ride bikes.

Arnold   Play ball and ride bikes. That sounds nice. What else?

Eddie *hesitates.*

Arnold   What else?

Eddie   Just stuff. I don't know. I don't want to talk about my kid.

Arnold   Will you teach me how to ride a bike?

Eddie   You can't ride a bike?

Arnold   I can't ride a bike.

Eddie   You never learned?

Arnold   I just said I can't ride a bike.

Eddie   We go camping sometimes.

Arnold   Just the two of you?

Eddie   Sometimes.

Arnold   My old man'd piss his pants.

Eddie   With the Boy Scouts.

Arnold   You're a Boy Scout?

Eddie   Scout Leader. For the Cub Scouts. (**Eddie** *realises he's revealed too much.*) Look, we should go.

Arnold   We haven't finished talking. You go camping with the Cub Scouts?

Eddie   Yes.

Arnold   You ever cop a feel on one of them?

Eddie   No!

Arnold   Not ever?

Eddie   No.

Arnold   What's stopping you?

Eddie   They're little kids. They're nice little boys.

Arnold   I'm a nice little boy.

Eddie   Right.

Arnold *retreats. After a moment.*

Arnold   You sleep in tents?

Eddie   Sometimes we sleep under the stars.

Arnold   You can't see any stars in the city.

Eddie   We go out to New Jersey. Pennsylvania sometimes.

Arnold   You can see the stars there?

Eddie   Yeah. What, you've never seen stars before?

Arnold   Nope.

Eddie   That's sad.

Arnold   That's not sad. It's just the way it is. Not everybody's got a dad who does shit with them. People survive. They grow up all the same. Don't give me 'that's sad' bullshit. You're sad. You're pathetic.

Eddie   You sure know how to make a person feel good.

Arnold   Take me camping.

Eddie   No.

Arnold   I want to go camping. With you and your kid.

Eddie   You can't.

Arnold   Why not? You embarrassed? You ashamed?

Eddie   You're too old to be a Cub Scout.

Arnold   Then make me a fucking Boy Scout.

Eddie   It's not that easy.

Arnold   You're the fucking Scout Leader. You telling me you don't have the power to make me a Boy Scout?

Eddie   You have to earn it.

Arnold   I can earn it. You tell me what to do. I'll earn it.

Eddie   It takes time.

Arnold   Then put me on the accelerated programme, bitch.

Eddie   I don't want sick shits like you around my kid.

Arnold   Don't tell me I can't.

He stands on the hood of the truck and screams.

Arnold   Help! Help me!

Eddie *grabs his leg and pulls him down.*

Eddie   You're gonna get us busted. Shut up.

Arnold   Help me!

Eddie   Goddamn it. Don't do that.

Arnold   Why can't I? I want to hear you say it.

Eddie   Because.

Arnold   Talk to me, Eddie. Talk, you fucker.

Eddie *doesn't speak.* **Arnold** *starts to scream again.*

Eddie   Because I don't like you, Arnold.

Arnold   Bastard.

Eddie   I think you're a freak.

Arnold   You can't get rid of me that easily, Eddie! What are you so afraid of?

Eddie   Leave me alone.

Arnold   Because you're ashamed.

Eddie   Yes.

Arnold   Because you don't want your wife to know.

Eddie   Yes.

Arnold   Because you're afraid you might like it?

Dead silence.

I'm right.

Pause.

Eddie   You've got it all figured out, don't you? You crazy fuck. Is this the only way you can get anyone to talk to you? By ruining their lives? You're just a pathetic little whore.

There is silence.

Arnold   Take me to the ferry. I want to go home. (**Arnold** *gets in the truck and slams the door.*) Now!

End of scene.

Scene Five

The garage. **Marie** *is heard from inside the house.*

Marie (*offstage*)   I'm sorry, what's your name again?

They enter.

Arnold   Arnold.

Marie   And Eddie's expecting you?

Arnold   Told me to stop by whenever.

Marie   You called the other day?

Arnold   Yeah. Eddie around?

Marie   On his way home. Are you sure Eddie's expecting you?

Arnold   Yeah.

Marie   It's just that Eddie didn't mention anything.

Arnold   He never talked about me before?

Marie   No.

Arnold   Can't believe he never said anything. Eddie, he's a great guy.

Arnold *paces around, casually scoping things out. He examines the cabinet doors.*

Marie   Careful. Sorry, it's just that Eddie's not finished with them.

Arnold   He build those?

Marie   Yes.

Arnold   They're nice.

Marie   Look, I need to start dinner.

Arnold   What for?

Marie   I have to cook dinner.

Arnold   The cabinets.

Marie   We're just trying to fix the place up.

Arnold   That's cool.

Arnold *continues to poke around. He finds a Cub Scout hat and puts it on.*

Marie   That's Eddie's.

Arnold   Yeah, he said he'd get me one. For the camp-out this weekend.

Marie   You're a Boy Scout?

Arnold   Eddie's going to teach me. About camping and making a fire. You know.

Marie (*somewhat relieved*)   Yes. The camping trip.

Arnold   My old man, he doesn't do stuff like that. So Eddie said he'd take me.

Marie   Of course.

Eddie *enters offstage.*

Eddie (*offstage*)   I'm home. Marie?

Marie (*yelling*)   Out here.

Eddie *enters.*

Eddie   I'm starving. What's for dinner?

He notices **Arnold**. **Eddie** *is speechless.*

Marie   Lasagna.

Arnold   Hi, Eddie.

Marie   You didn't tell me you were taking Arnold camping.

Arnold   Like we talked about.

Eddie   Yeah, yeah, yeah. Camping.

Arnold   I never even been out of the city.

Marie   You should have told me earlier, Eddie. The Women's League might have been able to donate some camping gear. I'll call Nick and see if Arnold can borrow Bobby's tent since he's not going.

Eddie   That'd be great. You go on in and call Nick.

Marie *exits.*

Arnold   Like my hat?

Eddie *rips the hat off* **Arnold**'*s head.*

Eddie   You think you're funny.

Arnold *tries to get the hat back.*

Arnold   You trashed my hat. Seems only fair.

Eddie   Forget the hat.

Arnold   I'm going camping.

Eddie   No you're not.

Arnold   We gonna sing around the camp fire?

Eddie   What did you tell her?

Arnold   What do you want me to tell her?

Eddie   You're in my house now. You don't fuck with a man in his own house.

Arnold   You won't let me, remember?

Eddie   I mean it. You don't say a word.

Arnold   Or what?

Eddie Don't tempt me.

Arnold She thinks I'm some charity case. Relax. Unless you want me to tell her the truth. 'Cause I can.

Marie (*yells from offstage*) Nick's here.

Eddie Keep your mouth shut.

Arnold I just want to go camping. Why you got to go complicating things?

Nick *enters.*

Nick McKale's has two-dollar pints tonight. My treat.

Marie (*yells from offstage*) Ask him about the tent.

Nick What's up? You can't find all your stuff?

Eddie No. We got everything.

Nick (*to* **Arnold**) Hi.

Arnold I'm Arnold. Eddie's friend.

Nick A friend of Eddie's. (*To* **Eddie**.) Whatcha been doing? Hanging around the arcade?

Eddie *is clearly not amused.*

Arnold Eddie's taking me camping. Right, Eddie?

Nick You look a little big to be a Cub Scout.

Arnold I'm a Boy Scout. Right, Eddie?

Marie *enters with a sleeping bag. It's a kid's sleeping bag.*

Marie You ask him about the tent?

Nick Sure. You can borrow it.

Marie I found Eddie Jr.'s old sleeping bag. Hope you don't mind the cartoons. It's pretty warm. Might be a little short for you though.

Arnold (*to* **Nick**) Eddie, he was nice enough to invite me along.

Nick What a swell guy.

Eddie Unless his old man says he can't.

Arnold No, I asked. It's fine. Really. He works a lot. Doesn't really have time for stuff, you know?

Nick So what, it's like some Big Brother kinda thing?

Eddie Something like that.

Marie You didn't tell me you were gonna be a Big Brother.

Eddie Must have forgot (*To* **Arnold**.) You got a way home tonight?

Arnold No.

Nick You coming down to McKale's?

Eddie I should drive the kid home.

Arnold I got a name.

Nick You sure man? My treat.

Arnold Maybe I don't want you to drive me home.

Eddie It's late. You don't want to be on the ferry this late.

Marie Let him drive you home.

Eddie I'll catch up with you guys later.

Nick You know where to find us.

Nick *exits*.

Marie What about dinner?

Eddie I'm gonna drive him back into the city.

Marie He can stay.

Eddie He's not staying! I said he could go camping. He's not having dinner with the family.

Marie Don't snap at me. I was just offering.

Eddie Well, don't.

Arnold I'll take the ferry.

Eddie No.

Marie When are you going to be home?

Eddie When I get home. (*To* **Arnold**.) Get in the truck.

Marie Don't be late. I need you to take Eddie to school in the morning.

Eddie You're telling me now?

Marie Didn't know I had to book ahead.

Eddie I got a job in the morning.

Marie So do I. You're looking at the new lunch manager.

Eddie When were you going to tell me?

Marie At dinner, but now you're going out drinking with Nick.

Eddie See, this is what I'm talking about, Marie. One day a week was one thing. Now you're going to be gone all day.

Marie Not all day. Training tomorrow, then I'll start working lunches, eleven to two. Three hours, Eddie. That's all. I'll make good money.

Eddie Hope the Women's League is worth it.

Marie You're not gonna say no to me.

Eddie Would it do any good?

Marie I'm not having this discussion right now. Take the kid to the ferry. I'll get Debbie to walk Eddie to the bus. Forget about it. Arnold, nice meeting you.

Eddie Get in the truck.

Marie Don't stay out late. Please.

Eddie I won't.

Marie   You're already tired.

Eddie   Would you please give me my balls back?

Marie   Fine.

Eddie   Thank you. I'll be home.

Eddie *gets in the truck and cranks the engine.*

End of scene.

Scene Six

Later that night. **Eddie** *and* **Arnold** *are at the dump.*

Arnold   I thought you were taking me home.

Eddie   How fucking dare you.

Arnold   That's no way to talk to a guest, Eddie. I'm offended.

Eddie   You can't do that, Arnold. You can't go showing up at my house.

Arnold   I think Marie likes me. Or she just feels sorry for me. You know, me being underprivileged and all.

Eddie   I oughta turn you in to the cops.

Arnold   And tell them what?

Eddie   You're stalking me.

Arnold   And I tell them how this big old man has lured me off the internet. How he makes me touch him 'down there'. Kisses me. Talks dirty. Then Marie will find out and it'll all just be one big mess. See what I mean, Eddie?

Eddie   You've got this all planned out, don't you?

Arnold   Doesn't really take planning, Eddie. It's just the way it is.

Eddie   What do you want from me?

Arnold We've been over this, Eddie. You're not listening to me. I want to go camping with the Boy Scouts. I want you. To take me. Camping. Now that's not so hard, is it?

Eddie You're not my responsibility.

Arnold Haven't you heard that old speech about how it takes a village? Eddie, you are my village.

Eddie I take you camping and you walk away.

Arnold I didn't say that.

Eddie That's what I'm offering. I take you camping and you walk out of my life. Don't look back.

Arnold I don't know if I like that deal.

Eddie Do it. I take you camping.

Arnold You teach me how to build a fire and put up a tent and shit?

Eddie All that.

Arnold And you tuck me in at night?

Eddie You sleep in your own tent.

Arnold But what if I get scared?

Eddie You're a big boy, Arnold.

Arnold Fine.

Eddie Deal.

Arnold But don't fuck up, Eddie.

There is a pause. A sigh of relief from **Eddie**. **Eddie** *starts to crank the engine.*

Arnold Wait.

Eddie I gotta get home.

Arnold Can we just sit?

Eddie No.

Arnold   Yes! Please?

Eddie *gives in. They sit in silence. Finally.*

Arnold   Thank you, Eddie.

Silence.

Eddie *finally relaxes.* **Arnold** *slowly runs his hand between* **Eddie**'s *legs.* **Eddie** *tries to push him away.*

Eddie   Stop it.

Arnold   Relax, Eddie. It feels good, doesn't it?

Eddie   This is not part of the deal.

Arnold   Think of it as a bonus.

Eddie *lets out a moan.*

Arnold   I want to make you feel good. You like it, right? Say you like it, Eddie.

Arnold *unbuttons* **Eddie**'s *pants.*

Eddie   No.

Arnold   Don't talk.

Arnold *massages* **Eddie**. *He then leans down. All we see is the look on* **Eddie**'s *face. Just as* **Eddie** *reaches climax, a bright light shines through the window.*

Eddie   Fuck!

End of Act One.

Act Two

Scene One

The garage. 2 a.m. The truck is missing from the garage. **Eddie** *sits at the card table.* **Nick** *paces back and forth.*

Nick *pops* **Eddie** *on the back of the head.*

Nick You're lucky I didn't leave your sorry ass down there. Them boys at Rikers party hard. Especially with sick fucks like you.

Eddie It's not . . .

Nick *pops him again.*

Nick Uh-uh. Not your turn yet. (**Nick** *continues to pace, unable to speak.*) Well?

Eddie It was all a misunderstanding.

Nick *pops him again.*

Nick Don't give me that shit.

Eddie Would you stop hitting me? I'm not some asshole you pulled in off the street.

Nick You're right. You're my brother-in-law. My sister's husband, who got pulled in for getting sucked off by a male prostitute.

Eddie He's not a prostitute.

Nick Excuse me if I got my facts wrong. The kid had a record, Eddie. You know that? About a mile long. Shop-lifting. Possession. Extortion. You know anything about that extortion charge?

Eddie No.

Nick You sure, Eddie? 'Cause that extortion charge has a restraining order attached to it. Some guy out in Queens.

Eddie   I didn't know!

Nick   Bet you didn't know his dad's some big shot investment banker either. This street kid routine's a bunch of bullshit. He played you, Eddie.

Eddie   How was I supposed to know?

Nick   The boys cut him lose. Didn't tell his probation officer. Told him to stay far, far away.

Eddie   Thanks for getting me out.

Nick   You better fucking thank me. You better get down on your knees and thank God that you are sitting here with me right now. 'Cause let me tell you, Eddie, I'm your own personal messiah.

Eddie   We talked online. That's it. Then he starts sending me these e-mails. And pictures of himself. I try deleting them but he sends me more. Then he's calling me. And showing up here. I told him to go away.

Nick   You told him to go away. Well, good for you. Something made you look, Eddie. Something made you write back.

Eddie   He's blackmailing me. It's like he gets off on it.

Nick   And what about you? You get off on it?

Eddie   Nick?

Nick *is on the verge of tears.*

Nick   You sick fucking son of a bitch. What do I do, Eddie? You tell me. You're married to my sister. You're my son's godfather. You're my friend, Eddie. My fucking oldest friend in the world. And you go and mess that all up. What's the matter, Eddie? Marie not good enough for you?

Eddie   I love Marie. I have always loved Marie. You know that.

Nick   She ever finds out it'll destroy her.

Eddie   She's not going to find out. Right, Nick?

Nick   What are you gonna tell her about the truck?

Eddie   I'll get it back this afternoon.

Nick   I'm not giving you money.

Eddie   I didn't ask you to.

Nick   What's to stop me from walking in there and telling her?

Eddie   She'll take Eddie away.

Nick   You don't deserve to be his father.

Eddie   And he doesn't deserve to grow up without one. Nick, please. Don't ruin that for him.

Nick   You been messing with Eddie Jr.?

Eddie   I'm not some paedophile.

Nick   Cause if I find out you been messing with that kid I swear to God, Eddie, I'll cut your dick off myself.

Eddie   Stop being so holier-than-thou. You're no saint.

Nick   I'm not getting head from no sixteen-year-old punk. You gay, Eddie?

Eddie   No.

Nick   You a faggot?

Eddie   Are you?

Nick   Fuck you.

Eddie   You never minded when Stanley Bianco sucked you off after we won a football game.

Nick   Hey! You don't talk about that. Nobody talks about that.

Eddie   Why? 'Cause you made a mistake? Because it didn't mean anything?

Nick   Clearly you were digging it.

Eddie   Didn't seem to think it was so bad then.

Nick   Stanley Bianco blew half the football team. It's just different.

Eddie   Why?

Nick   'Cause it was high school. 'Cause we were stupid.

Eddie   Because it was a warm place to stick your dick. Because it was exciting. Because it felt good. Because your girlfriend or your wife wouldn't do it. Or resented doing it. (*Pause.*) Nick, I fucked up.

Nick   You fucked up? Fucking up is screwing some drunk broad down at McKale's. News flash for you Eddie. Marriage is messy. It's finding pubic hair on the toilet seat and not caring. You get past it. You don't go fucking punk kids you pick up on the internet.

Eddie   They gonna put me in jail, Nick?

Nick   I had to call in a lifetime's worth of favours to make this one disappear.

Eddie   I can't take jail.

Nick   Don't think I'm doing this for you.

Eddie   I'll do whatever you want me to, Nick. Just tell me.

Nick   Here's the deal, Eddie. You're gonna get rid of this kid. For good, you hear me? I don't care how. I won't ask questions. Then you're gonna start worshipping the ground my sister walks on, understood? I want you voted fucking husband of the year. And if I find out you so much as think about him I'll bust your ass. I'm watching you, Eddie.

End of Scene.

Scene Two

6 a.m. The cabinets are gone, except for one which **Eddie** *is assembling. He is dressed from the previous scene and hasn't slept all night.*

There is a shriek from inside.

Marie   Oh my God! Eddie! Eddie!

Marie *enters. She is in her pyjamas.*

Eddie   You OK?

Marie   Eddie, they're beautiful.

Eddie   You like them?

Marie   They're amazing.

Marie *gives* **Eddie** *a kiss.*

Eddie   I'm almost finished with this one.

Marie   You didn't have to do that.

Eddie   I wanted to. I promised. I like to see you happy.

Marie *puts her arms around him, nuzzling his neck.*

Marie   They're perfect.

Eddie   If you don't like the colour I can re-stain them.

Marie   I said, they're perfect.

Eddie   I wanted to finish them before we leave tomorrow. You gotta have nice cabinets when you have the Women's League over, right? Want the house to look nice.

Marie   You stayed up all night?

Eddie   Couldn't sleep.

Marie   You must be exhausted.

Eddie   I'm holding up.

Marie   You want me to make you some coffee?

Eddie I've had a pot already.

Marie *picks up the coffee cup.*

Marie It's ice cold. I'll make you some fresh.

Eddie No. I'm OK. Really.

Marie *and* **Eddie** *kiss.*

Marie You surprise me sometimes.

Eddie What?

Marie Just you.

Eddie I've just been thinking about it, and you're right. The Women's League, they'd be real good for you.

Marie Thank you.

Eddie You do all this work here at home, taking care of Eddie Jr. You're real good with him, Marie. I don't think I ever told you that. You're a good mother.

Marie Eddie, I'm gonna cry.

Eddie Don't do that. Don't cry.

Marie It's just I feel like sometimes I got nobody to talk to. About, you know – woman things. It's hard.

Eddie Well, you tell those ladies down at the Women's League they'd be pretty stupid to pass you over. You'd be the best thing they've ever had.

Eddie *kisses* **Marie** *again.*

Eddie How much are these ladies gonna need to make you a member?

Marie It's like dues spread out over a year. Plus community service.

Eddie You just let me know how much.

Marie I got my job now.

Eddie   Tell them no. I don't want my wife working all the time. We'll find the money, OK?

Marie   I can't. I can't tell them no. I gotta take this. Not just for the money, but for me. I like working.

Eddie   Please.

Marie   You gotta understand.

Eddie   No, I get it. You need anything, Marie, you tell me. I'll get it for you, OK? You change your mind, you know, about working. That's OK, too.

Marie   OK.

Eddie   OK. They need the money now?

Marie   I'm not a member yet.

Eddie   'Cause I need to take two hundred and fifty bucks out of our account.

Marie   What for?

Eddie   It's a surprise.

Marie   We can't afford surprises.

Eddie   I was thinking maybe we'd go to Atlantic City next weekend.

Marie   We can't afford Atlantic City.

Eddie   I got a buddy who can get us a room for free. Just you and me. And a Jacuzzi in the bathroom big enough for two. Some candles. A little music in the background. Nick and Debbie said they'd keep Eddie Jr.

Marie   If it's free what do you need two hundred and fifty dollars for?

Eddie   That's part of the surprise.

Eddie *kisses her passionately.* **Marie** *pulls away.*

Marie   What's that about?

Eddie   I like kissing you. Remember when we used to wake up early in the morning and make love? Start the day feeling high?

Marie   I gotta get ready for work and make Eddie's lunch.

Eddie   He can buy his lunch today.

He runs his hands up her shirt.

Marie   I gotta get Eddie dressed.

Eddie   We got a few minutes. I'll get him dressed while you make his lunch.

Marie   God knows what he'd look like.

Eddie   I got style.

Eddie *bends down and kisses her breast.* **Marie** *giggles.*

Eddie   That's nice.

Marie   My breasts are nice?

Eddie   Hearing you laugh.

Marie   It tickles.

Eddie   Oh yeah?

Eddie *kisses the other side.* **Marie** *lets out another laugh.*

Marie   Stop, stop, stop.

Marie *notices the truck is missing.*

Marie   Where'd you park the truck?

Eddie   Nick drove me home last night.

Marie   You got too drunk to drive? Nice, Eddie. Real nice.

Eddie   I'll go get it this afternoon.

Marie   You remember where you parked it at least?

Eddie   Right where I left it.

Marie You got towed. That's your surprise?

Eddie It's not my fault.

Marie We're already running short this month.

Eddie I'll have the money back in the bank by Monday.

Marie And how are you going to do that?

Eddie I got that check from the drywall coming in. I'll call and tell them I gotta pick it up today. Then I'll take you to Atlantic City.

Marie (*sarcastically*) And everything'll be OK.

Eddie Would you cut me some slack? I'm trying. Don't get upset. Please. I built your cabinets, just like you like them. Don't ruin it.

Silence. **Eddie** *goes to* **Marie**.

Eddie I love you. I don't ever want to lose you.

Marie I'm not going anywhere.

Eddie Promise.

Marie What's this about? Are you sick? You're not dying, are you?

Eddie No.

Marie You're being so dramatic.

Eddie Do you still love me?

Marie Of course.

Eddie Tell me.

Marie I love you.

Eddie Really?

Marie I love you. OK?

Eddie Promise me?

Marie   Promise. Now come on. I need to get Eddie up.

Marie *pulls away.*

Eddie   So I'll take the money out this afternoon.

Marie   You gotta have the truck.

Eddie   And then I'll take you to Atlantic City. Just the two of us.

Marie   You get yourself paid for that drywall job.

Marie *exits.*

End of Scene.

Scene Three

The dump. Friday night. **Arnold** *looks anxious.*

Arnold   Look man, this place is creeping me out.

Eddie   But this is our special place, right?

Arnold   Are you stupid? They're probably watching this place. Taking pictures and shit, waiting to bust our asses.

Eddie   We aren't doing anything.

Arnold   You think they care about that?

Eddie   You worried?

Arnold   No.

Eddie   They cut you loose last night.

Arnold   Still.

Eddie   I thought you might like being locked up with a bunch of bad asses like you. Can't play with the big boys?

Arnold   I'm a minor, man. I'm golden for two more years.

Eddie   Aren't you lucky?

Arnold Why you got so much attitude? They didn't hold you.

Eddie No, I just got strip-searched and questioned for three hours. You ever been strip-searched? Stripped naked and told to bend over?

Arnold I didn't tell them nothing. They let you go. Come on, Eddie, don't be mad at me.

Eddie Don't be mad at you? I'm a little more than just mad.

Arnold I thought it's what you wanted. Look, I'm sorry. Really. Please.

He retreats for a moment. He then pulls two Mets hats out of his backpack.

Arnold I got you something.

He hands **Eddie** *the hat.*

Arnold Take it. It's a present. I got me one too. So we can match. Maybe we could go to a game sometime?

Eddie You buy this with your allowance?

Arnold Please. I want you to have it. Take it, man.

Eddie You steal it?

Arnold I jacked it from this store in Times Square, OK? I just wanted to give you something.

Eddie Your daddy didn't buy it for you?

Arnold My old man doesn't give me the time of day.

Eddie I know you got money. This street kid routine go over well at your little private school?

Arnold You don't know nothing about it.

Eddie You owe me two hundred and fifty bucks.

Arnold You're crazy.

Eddie   Cost me that much to get my truck back. Or maybe your dad'll pick up the tab.

Arnold   I don't owe you shit.

Eddie   Plus a ticket for trespassing.

Arnold   Not my fault you picked this place. Who the hell hangs out at the dump?

Eddie   That's where you take trash.

Arnold   Fuck you.

Silence.

I thought you liked it last night.

Eddie   Except for that minor interruption.

Arnold   So you did. You liked it.

Arnold *moves in towards* **Eddie**.

Arnold   We could try again.

Eddie   That's not what I meant. Why's it always gotta be about that?

Arnold   Me and you, that's what we are to each other, right?

Eddie   Don't be late tomorrow.

Arnold   You're taking me?

Eddie   Seven a.m. You're late and I leave without you.

Arnold   I'll be there, OK.

Eddie   This is it, Arnold. We get back and you walk away.

Arnold   I know.

Eddie   You promised.

Arnold   Why you freaking out? I know.

Eddie *pushes* **Arnold**.

Eddie   Get back on your side.

Arnold   What, I can't sit next to you? Chill, man.

Eddie   I don't want you touching me.

Arnold   Didn't seem to mind last night.

Eddie   I went home last night and took a shower for like an hour.

Arnold   I ain't got cooties.

Eddie   No telling where your mouth's been.

Arnold's *anger starts to grow.*

Arnold   On your dick.

Eddie   You make me feel dirty.

Arnold   I ain't dirty. You're dirty. A dirty bastard. I ain't gonna touch you, OK? Happy?

Eddie   Just keep your hands to yourself.

Arnold   I just wanted to sit by you. Can't even sit by you without you going all ape-shit on me. Can't I just sit by you? Just be close. I like just being close sometimes.

He slowly moves over closer to **Eddie**, *almost childlike.* **Arnold** *looks out the window.*

They sit in silence.

Arnold   See? Sometimes all people really need is to be close to someone.

End of scene.

Scene Four

Saturday morning. The last cabinet door has been hung. **Marie** *has dressed* **Arnold** *in a pair of khaki trouserss, dress shirt and tie. It's a sharp contrast to his baggy jeans and T-shirt.* **Marie** *is dressed up as well.*

Marie You look so handsome.

Arnold *pulls at his tie.*

Arnold I can't breathe.

Marie Don't. You'll mess it up.

Arnold I look like some Wall Street stiff.

Marie You look nice.

Arnold You think so?

Marie Come on. I bet all the girls at school are dying to go out with you.

Arnold Yeah.

Marie Wait till Eddie see you. He's going to be so impressed. (*Yells.*) Eddie, come see Arnold.

Arnold I really appreciate the new clothes.

Marie It's nothing.

Arnold No, really. You and Eddie, you've been real nice to me. Makes me feel like part of the family.

Marie Of course.

Eddie *enters with an ice chest.*

Eddie We're gonna have to pick up more ice. The ice-maker's on the blink again.

Marie Doesn't Arnold look nice?

Eddie What did you do to him?

Marie He looks nice, right?

Eddie What's he doing dressed like that?

Arnold Marie's going to introduce me to the Women's League.

Eddie What for?

Marie I just thought it would be nice for them to see that we, as a family, like to reach out to others. That we have a welcoming home.

Eddie We're leaving soon.

Marie But the ladies are on their way over. It's just for a minute.

Eddie We're leaving, Marie. Arnold, go change clothes.

Marie You can wait half an hour.

Eddie We're gonna be late.

Arnold But Marie worked so hard. She got me new clothes and everything.

Marie Nick's on his way over with the tent. You can't leave without a tent for Arnold.

Eddie We can pick up a tent on the way there.

Marie Nick's not using his. He's gonna walk it over.

Eddie You shouldn't have done that.

Marie Well, Arnold needs a tent. He can't sleep outside.

Arnold I could sleep with you.

Marie It's no big deal. (*To* **Arnold**.) Arnold, would you like some cereal? It's going to be a long drive to the camp.

Arnold Please.

Marie *exits.*

Arnold You look like shit.

Eddie Imagine that.

Arnold *picks up a huge camping knife and starts carving at a piece of wood.*

Eddie   Be careful with the knife, OK.

Arnold   I know what I'm doing. Not like I'm gonna go running through the house or nothing.

Eddie   All I need is for you to lose a finger or something.

Arnold   It's a cool knife.

Eddie   Put it down.

Marie *re-enters with a bowl of cereal.*

Marie   Be careful not to spill.

Marie *grabs a paper towel and tucks it into* **Arnold**'*s shirt like a bib.*

Eddie   He can feed himself. He doesn't need a bib.

Marie   I just don't want him to mess up his new shirt.

Arnold   Thank you.

Marie   The sky looks clear. You boys should have a good night for watching the stars.

Arnold   I hope so.

Eddie   I said, put it down, Arnold.

Marie   Watch the boys with that thing.

Eddie   I'll have it with me the whole time.

Marie   I'm glad Arnold's going with you. It'll be good to have another set of eyes looking after the boys.

Nick *calls from the living room.*

Nick (*offstage*)   Marie!

Marie   Out here.

Nick *enters with the extra tent.*

Nick   Stuff's all there.

Marie   Thanks for walking it over. Did you see my cabinets? They look beautiful.

Nick   No, I didn't see them.

Marie   You gotta look before you leave. Eddie stayed up all night making them perfect.

Nick   Arnold. Eddie, you didn't tell me Arnold was still going on the camping trip.

Eddie   Gave him my word.

Nick   See you got the truck back.

Marie   I'm gonna string you both up if it happens again.

Nick   I'm not his keeper.

Arnold   What happened to your truck, Eddie?

Eddie *glares at* **Arnold**.

Marie   Yeah, Eddie, tell him what happened? Tell him how you got drunk and the truck got towed. Some kind of example you're setting.

Eddie   I got it back, didn't I? No harm done.

Marie   Tell that to the bank when we're late on the mortgage this month.

Eddie   You're the one buying Arnold new clothes.

Marie   Arnold, why don't you change? You'll just have to come back another time and meet the Women's League.

Marie *and* **Arnold** *exit to the house.*

Nick *and* **Eddie** *pause while they wait for them to get inside.*

Nick   That's what you told her? It got towed while we was out drinking?

Eddie   It worked.

Nick   You testing me? You think I won't keep my promise? 'Cause let me tell you, the ice is getting thin.

Eddie   No, I know.

Nick   Are you fucking crazy?

Eddie   Listen . . .

Nick   'Cause if you're crazy, then I can handle that. They got special places for crazy people. But right now I'm thinking you're just plain stupid. You didn't hear a goddamn word I said.

Eddie   Be quiet man, she'll hear you.

Nick   She's gonna hear me all right. The whole damn town's gonna hear soon. You want that? You trying to break her heart? That what it is?

Eddie   I got a plan, Nick.

Nick   Oh, I'm sure you do.

Eddie   I'm going to take the kid camping.

Nick   You're gonna let this freak spend the weekend with Eddie Jr.?

Eddie   I'm thinking Arnold might get lost in the woods.

Nick *takes a moment to think about this.*

Nick   Lost in the woods.

Eddie   He's a city kid. Makes sense he won't know how to find his way out. Parents probably won't even miss him. I know I won't.

Nick   When I said get rid of him, this isn't what I had in mind.

Pause.

Cover your tracks, man.

Eddie   I'm just going to scare the kid.

Nick   I'm just saying.

Marie *and* **Arnold** *enter.* **Arnold** *is in his Boy Scout shirt and shorts.*

Marie   You sure you can't wait a little longer?

Eddie   For the last time, Marie. No.

Nick   I better get going.

Eddie   You still up for keeping the kid next weekend?

Nick   Sure.

Eddie *pulls a cheque out of his pocket and hands it to* **Marie**.

Eddie   Cause me and Marie, we're going to Atlantic City.

Marie   You got paid!

Eddie   Went by yesterday afternoon and told them I had to have the money. My buddy got us a room.

Nick   No problem. You be careful out there.

Arnold   Thanks for the tent.

Nick   Do what Eddie tells you.

Arnold   Always.

Nick *exits.*

Arnold   I've always wanted to go to Atlantic City.

Eddie (*to* **Arnold**)   Put the ice chest in the truck. Marie, get Eddie Jr.

Arnold *just stands there.*

Arnold   No one's ever taken me to Atlantic City before.

Eddie   Now, Arnold.

Marie   You're too young to go to Atlantic City.

Arnold   I could watch Eddie Jr. while you guys are at the casino. We could hang out at the beach and stuff.

Marie   That's awfully sweet of you, Arnold. It's just that me and Eddie need some time alone together.

Arnold   I get it.

Marie   Couples need that sometimes.

Eddie   Put the goddamn ice chest in the truck.

Arnold   No, I know. Right, Eddie? Couples need some time together. Alone.

Eddie (*to* **Marie**)   Go get Eddie Jr. ready. We're going to be late.

Arnold   So I guess this is it, Big Brother. You've done your duty. Time to move on.

Marie   No, not at all. Maybe the next weekend you can come and spend some time? Have dinner.

Eddie   Now!

Marie   Or maybe you could come over when Eddie Jr. has his next Cub Scout meeting.

Eddie   He's not coming back.

Marie   Eddie . . .

Eddie   Arnold's not coming back here. I said so.

Marie   You're the one who brought him here. You can't just make a commitment to someone and not see it through.

Arnold   She's right.

Marie   We'll talk about it later. I'm going to get Eddie dressed.

Arnold *follows* **Marie**.

Eddie   You stay here. I don't want you near him.

Marie   Arnold didn't do anything.

Eddie   Trust me, Marie.

Arnold You hate me, don't you?

Marie Eddie doesn't hate you.

Eddie Stay out of it, Marie.

Arnold He doesn't want me around any more. Nobody wants me around.

Eddie You just figured that out?

Marie We want you around. Just not all the time.

Arnold We had a deal.

Eddie Get out of my house.

Arnold What'd I do?

Marie Eddie . . .

Eddie You come here into my house and eat breakfast with my wife. And pretend like you belong here. Well, you don't.

Arnold (*desperate*) You said you would take me camping. You promised.

Eddie Well, I'm breaking my promise. Get out.

Arnold You're just like my old man.

Eddie I'm sorry your father's a dick. I'm sorry nobody loves you. I'm sorry the world has shit on you. But you know what? It's not my fault. And you're not my responsibility.

Eddie *grabs* **Arnold** *by the shirt and tries to drag him to the door.* **Arnold** *pulls away.*

Arnold Don't touch me, man.

Eddie I don't want you anywhere near my family.

Marie Let go of him.

Arnold *starts to crumble.*

Arnold   Come on, Eddie. Don't make me leave.

Eddie   Go home, Arnold.

Arnold   Please, Eddie. I'll be good.

Eddie   You don't belong here.

Arnold   I won't do nothing wrong.

Eddie   You can't stay.

Arnold   I'll tell. You want me to tell her?

Marie   Tell me what?

Eddie   Shut your mouth.

Arnold   What do you think she'll say when she knows the truth?

Marie   What's he talking about?

Eddie   Don't listen to him, Marie.

Arnold   What's she going to say, Eddie?

Eddie   Go ahead. Go ahead.

Arnold *speaks to* **Marie**.

Arnold   What happened to Eddie's truck?

Marie   It got towed.

Arnold   Is that what you told her?

Eddie   It did.

Arnold   By the cops.

Eddie   So what?

Arnold   As evidence.

Eddie   You couldn't resist.

Marie   What's going on here?

Arnold Your husband likes to talk dirty. He talk dirty to you?

Marie What's he saying?

Arnold He likes it hard and fast.

Marie Eddie . . .

Arnold Did he ever tell you how he hates that you'll only have sex with the lights off?

Marie What?

Arnold How you can't look him in the eye while you fuck?

Marie Stop it . . .

Arnold How he wished you didn't worry about how you smelled . . .

Marie Make him stop.

Arnold That he wants you to lick his balls . . .

Marie You told him these things? About us. About you and me?

Arnold Bet I know more about him than you do.

Eddie I couldn't tell you.

Marie Why? Why, Eddie?

Eddie I didn't know . . . it was just . . .

Marie So you told a boy?

Eddie It wasn't real, Marie. It was like pretend.

Marie It's pretty real right now, Eddie.

Arnold He came to me. He needed me. I gave him those things.

Marie You had sex with him?

Eddie   No. We never.

Marie *starts piecing it together.*

Marie   The truck. In the truck.

Arnold   Busted.

Marie   Where you and me made love? You had sex with him.

Eddie   It wasn't really sex.

Marie   Did you?

Eddie   No.

Marie   Did you have sex with my husband? Answer me.

Arnold   No.

Marie   Tell me the truth.

Arnold   Yes.

Eddie   NO! He's lying.

Marie   Did he touch you?

Arnold   I touched him.

Eddie   But that's all.

Marie   You stand here and say that's all?

Eddie *tries to comfort her.*

Marie   Don't touch me.

Eddie   Please, Marie.

Marie   Get away from me. I want you out.

Eddie   Don't say that.

Marie   OUT! Out of my house. You think you'll ever see Eddie again?

Arnold picks up the knife and holds it to his throat.

Eddie   Don't do this. He's been stalking me. Ask Nick.

Marie   Nick knows?

Eddie   Tell her, Arnold. Tell the truth.

Eddie *and* **Marie** *see* **Arnold** *with the knife.*

Arnold   What about this, Eddie? Does this mean something?

Marie   Don't!

Arnold   You ever see anyone slit their own throat?

Marie   Put the knife down.

Arnold   Why?

Marie (*to* **Eddie**)   Get it away from him.

Eddie   If you died today would anybody miss you?

Arnold   Tell her you loved me.

Eddie   Would they?

Arnold   Tell her you wanted me.

Eddie   No one, right?

Arnold   Stop being mean.

Eddie   I'm not being mean, I'm being honest.

Marie   Stop it, Eddie.

Arnold   I trusted you.

Eddie   You make a mistake, you pay the consequences.

Marie   Get out.

Arnold   Don't come any closer. I'll do it.

Marie   Get out!

Eddie   No you won't.

Arnold   I will.

Eddie   She's going to leave me, Arnold. Marie's going to leave and take Eddie Jr. with her. And there's going to be one more kid in this world with no father to take him camping.

Arnold   Good.

Eddie   And if they lock me up, we can't be together either.

Arnold   They won't do that.

Eddie   They might.

Arnold   No.

Eddie   Tell her the truth, Arnold.

Arnold   I'm sorry.

Eddie   Tell her I didn't touch you. Tell her it was all just a game.

Marie   You think it's a game?

Arnold   It was more than that, Eddie. Don't you see? You mean something to me.

Eddie   It all went wrong.

Arnold   Please. I'm so sorry. He loves you. He loves your little boy. He told me.

Marie *starts to cry softly.* **Eddie** *picks up the portable phone.*

Eddie   I do, Marie. I love you both.

Eddie *pulls out a slip of paper and dials the phone.*

Arnold   What are you doing?

Eddie   I'm calling your father.

Arnold   Where'd you get that?

Eddie   Found it.

Arnold   You're not calling my parents.

Eddie   You need them. More than you need me.

Arnold No. They'll send me away.

Eddie You need help.

Arnold I can't go to one of those places.

Eddie You can't stay here.

Arnold Why are you doing this?

Eddie Because if you were my kid, I'd want someone to call.

Arnold Like he's gonna care.

Eddie Give him a chance.

Arnold You're bluffing.

Eddie Game's over, Arnold.

Arnold Please.

There is silence.

Eddie Is this Arnold's father? Hi. My name is Eddie.

Arnold *slits his throat.* **Marie** *screams.* **Eddie** *drops the phone.*

End of play.